AUG 2019

Katharine Blodgett
and Invisible Glass

By Virginia Loh-Hagan

21st Century
Junior Library

Published in the United States of America by
Cherry Lake Publishing
Ann Arbor, Michigan
www.cherrylakepublishing.com

Content Adviser: Kirsten Edwards, MA, Educational Studies
Reading Adviser: Marla Conn, MS, Ed., Literacy specialist, Read-Ability, Inc.

Photo Credits: © Ben Schonewille/Shutterstock.com, Cover, 1; © Natalia Lebedinskaia/Shutterstock.com, 4; © Syda Productions/ Shutterstock.com, 6; © tomertu/Shutterstock.com, 8; © Sergey Nivens/Shutterstock.com, 10; © Smithsonian Institution Archives/Image # SIA2007-0282, 12; © Evgeny Starkov/Shutterstock.com, 14; © tristan tan/Shutterstock.com, 16; © Jaromir Chalabala/Shutterstock.com, 18; © Onchira Wongsiri/Shutterstock.com, 20

Library of Congress Cataloging-in-Publication Data

Names: Loh-Hagan, Virginia, author.
Title: Katharine Blodgett and invisible glass / by Virginia Loh-Hagan.
Description: Ann Arbor : Cherry Lake Publisher, [2018] | Series: Women innovators |
    Includes bibliographical references and index. | Audience: Grades 4 to 6.
Identifiers: LCCN 2018003308| ISBN 9781534129160 (hardcover) | ISBN 9781534130869 (pdf) |
    ISBN 9781534132368 (pbk.) | ISBN 9781534134065 (hosted ebook)
Subjects: LCSH: Blodgett, Katharine B. (Katherine Burr), 1898-1979—Juvenile literature. | Women glassworkers—Biography—Juvenile
    literature. | Industrial chemists—United States—Biography—Juvenile literature. | Women chemists—United States—Biography—
    Juvenile literature. | Glass coatings—Juvenile literature. | Anti-reflective coatings—Juvenile literature.
Classification: LCC TP806.B55 L64 2018 | DDC 666/.1092 [B] —dc23
LC record available at https://lccn.loc.gov/2018003308

Cherry Lake Publishing would like to acknowledge the work of The Partnership for 21st Century Skills.
Please visit *www.p21.org* for more information.

Printed in the United States of America
Corporate Graphics

CONTENTS

Everything around you was invented by someone.

A Woman

Do you wear glasses? Do you look out car windows? Do you put photos in picture frames? All these things use a special type of glass. And this glass was invented by Katharine Blodgett.

Blodgett was an engineer and scientist. She's known for inventing non-**reflective** glass. This is also known as invisible glass. She came up with the process for how to make it.

Blodgett wrote, spoke, and read in
both English and French.

Blodgett was born on January 10, 1898, in Schenectady, New York. Her father was a famous **patent** lawyer. He worked for General Electric. He died unexpectedly.

Blodgett and her mother moved to France after his death. They later returned to New York. She got a better education than most girls of her time. She did really well in math and science.

Look!

Look around you. Make a list of things that are made of glass. Make a list of things that have glass parts.

Blodgett finished high school when she was only 15.

Blodgett was smart and got top grades. She was the first woman to get a **doctorate** in **physics** from Cambridge University in England.

She was also creative. She loved gardening and acting in plays. She collected old furniture and wrote funny poems. She was a member of the Zonta Club. This is a club of professional women that helps women all around the world. She died on October 12, 1979.

Mentors help people grow in their jobs and lives.

An Idea

Blodgett didn't have many options during her time. Most educated women became teachers. But Blodgett wanted to do more. She was the first female research scientist hired by General Electric. She worked there her whole life.

She was **mentored** by Irving Langmuir. Langmuir had also worked with her father. Blodgett learned a lot from him. They worked together on many projects.

Blodgett also worked with metal.

Blodgett built on Langmuir's work. She invented a way to apply **coatings** layer by layer to glass. She coated glass with a soapy **film**. These coatings were thin. Blodgett stacked the layers. She repeated her process. She layered the glass to a certain thickness. She worked very hard to be accurate. At a certain thickness, the layers remove any reflection.

Blodgett had created the world's first invisible glass. Her glass is **transparent**. Light passes through it, and no light is

Projectors and cameras use Blodgett's invisible glass.

reflected back. This makes it invisible. People can see clearly through the glass.

Blodgett and her invention were featured in many newspapers and magazines. She became a star. It was rare for women to be in science. Blodgett paved the way for other female scientists.

Ask Questions!

Ask someone to be your mentor. Ask questions about what they can teach you. Think about what you can learn from this person.

The first movie to use Blodgett's glass was
Gone with the Wind.

A Legacy

People used to have a hard time seeing through glass because the reflection was so strong. Blodgett changed that. Her **legacy** can be seen in the many inventions that benefited from her work. These include computer screens and telescopes. Her work is used in making movies. It was also used in World War II technology, like airplane spy cameras.

Blodgett invented ways to remove ice
from airplane wings.

Blodgett shared her knowledge. She wrote over 30 papers and helped other scientists. She invented more than invisible glass. She got eight patents. Getting patents was hard for women at this time.

Blodgett invented a way to measure the quality of glass. She also invented gear that could be used in war. She created **smoke screens** and gas masks. Her inventions saved thousands of soldiers' lives.

Blodgett also liked to act and write funny poems.

Blodgett got awards from many professional groups. She was also honored in the National Inventors Hall of Fame. Schenectady, New York, even created a Katharine Blodgett Day.

Blodgett was a new type of woman for her time. She didn't marry. She was independent. She chose science and her **career**. She was a role model for women.

Create!

Create your own day! What would you call this day? What activities would you plan for this day?

GLOSSARY

career (kuh-REER) a job or profession

coatings (KOH-tingz) thin layers or coverings of something

doctorate (DOK-ter-it) the highest degree awarded by a university

film (FILM) a thin layer covering something

legacy (LEG-uh-see) something handed down from one generation to another

mentored (MEN-tord) given advice and help by an experienced and trusted person

patent (PAT-uhnt) the right from the government to use or sell an invention for a certain number of years

physics (FIZ-iks) the study of matter and energy

reflective (rih-FLEK-tiv) able to send back light, energy, or sound from a surface

smoke screens (SMOHK SKREENZ) clouds of smoke created to hide military operations

transparent (tranz-PAIR-uhnt) allowing light to pass through so that objects behind can be clearly seen

FIND OUT MORE

BOOKS

Caldwell, Stella A. *100 Women Who Made History: Remarkable Women Who Shaped Our World*. New York: DK Publishing, 2017.

Ruzicka, Oldrich. *How Things Are Made*. New York: Sterling, 2016.

Thimmesh, Catherine. *Girls Think of Everything: Stories of Ingenious Inventions by Women*. Boston: Houghton Mifflin Company, 2000.

WEBSITES

Edison Tech Center—Katharine Burr Blodgett: Pioneer in Surface Chemistry and Engineering
www.edisontechcenter.org/Blodgett.html
Read this brief biography to learn more about Blodgett's life and achievements.

Mental Floss—19 Things You Might Not Know Were Invented by Women
http://mentalfloss.com/article/53164/19-things-you-might-not-know-were-invented-women
Read this list to learn about inventions made by women.

YouTube—Katharine Blodgett: Engineering Pioneer
https://www.youtube.com/watch?v=epnHUNngVz0
Watch this video in which Blodgett talks about her invention.

INDEX

ABOUT THE AUTHOR

Dr. Virginia Loh-Hagan is an author, university professor, former classroom teacher, and curriculum designer. She has visited Schenectady several times. She dedicates this book to the teachers she met there. She lives in San Diego with her very tall husband and very naughty dogs. To learn more about her, visit www.virginialoh.com.